For Agnes, Jamie, Pola, and Richard.
My Family.

Come, let us sing for joy to the LORD;
let us shout aloud to the Rock of our salvation.
Let us come before him with thanksgiving
and extol him with music and song.

Psalm 95:1-2

Contents

Hymns
In Chronological Order

Introduction

I first fell in love with hymns in 2017. My wife (then my fiancée), Agnes, and I were struggling to apply for her visa to live in the UK, so after our wedding she could join me in England. By this point we had spent seven years dating long-distance; I was in England and she was in Ohio.

I was also trying to prepare a home for us back in England. I was fruitlessly applying for a mortgage and searching for a house at the same time. Bank after bank was denying us any kind of mortgage. I was feeling incredibly disheartened and like I was failing Agnes. She was prepared to leave her home in Ohio but I couldn't provide her with a home in England.

In January 2018 we had the news that her visa had been denied and we had to appeal. They had scheduled a tribunal for us the following January, a whole year away. That May, we had our wedding in Ohio and Agnes came to England on a temporary visa. We bought my brother's flat from him as our first home and made it our own. Then in

October Agnes had to go back to the States and, because of financial commitments, I wasn't able to go with her.

During this time I had discovered a musician called Nathan Drake who had recorded acoustic versions of hymns. For the first time, I saw hymns as heart-felt worship and not out-of-date songs we unenthusiastically sung at church.

I started to use these hymns as personal worship. I would listen to them, learn them, and then sing them at home whilst playing my guitar. I was able to worship and encounter God in a new way.

Around that time we started a new evening service at church for a younger crowd.

Even though the service was aimed at younger church-goers, for one of the first services that I led I decided to only sing hymns. I had moaned for years about singing old hymns at church but now that I saw them in a new light I wanted to show my church, especially the teenagers, what I had learnt:

Hymns are as relevant today
as they were when they were written.

One common theme that has arisen from studying these hymns is that so many of them were written after a deep, personal encounter with God. Many of those encounters were after a tragedy. The hymn-writers were struggling with troubles and tragedies that are still prevalent today. They turned to God for comfort and safety and God was faithful to them and responded with love.

Even the oldest of hymns was written by someone who had encountered God and if Jesus Christ is the same yesterday and today and forever, as we're told in Hebrews 13:8, then the truth they learnt from that encounter is still relevant today.

Hymns allow us to have a shared experience of authentic faith from people who lived hundreds, and sometimes thousands, of years ago.

American pastor and author John Piper said:

"The inner essence of worship is to know God truly and then respond from the heart to that knowledge by valuing God, treasuring God, prizing God, enjoying God, being satisfied with God above all earthly things. And then that deep, restful, joyful satisfaction in God overflows in demonstrable acts of praise from the lips and demonstrable acts of love in serving others for the sake of Christ."

("What is Worship?" 2016)

This shows a process of natural worship:

- First we come to know who God is.
- Then we respond in our heart.
- Then we respond from our mouths, with prayer, preaching and praise.
- Then we respond with our actions, by demonstrating God's love through serving others.

A lot of these hymns are written as an oral response to experiencing God. We can use their words for our own worship. Read these hymns, listen to them, and learn them, so that when you experience God you can respond with praise.

But don't let your praise end there. After you praise God, go and worship through acts of love. Serve your friends, family, and neighbours. Show them who God is, show them who Christ is, show them what the Holy Spirit can do, by loving them and serving them so they can't help but know who God is.

William Long
Hertford, 2020

Hymns

Note

I have tried to use the original lyrics to the hymns but, as there are so many variations and minor differences between published versions, some may not be the author's original text. Where it was difficult to identify the original I chose the version that I felt best represented the author's intent.

The Magnificat

4BC - *approx.*

Words

Mary, Mother of Jesus

My soul magnifies the Lord,
and my spirit rejoices in God my Saviour,
for he has looked on the humble estate of his servant.
For behold, from now on all generations will call me blessed;
for he who is mighty has done great things for me,
and holy is his name.
And his mercy is for those who fear him
from generation to generation.

He has shown strength with his arm;
he has scattered the proud in the thoughts of their hearts;
he has brought down the mighty from their thrones
and exalted those of humble estate;
he has filled the hungry with good things,
and the rich he has sent away empty.

He has helped his servant Israel,
in remembrance of his mercy,
as he spoke to our fathers,
to Abraham and to his offspring forever.

Luke 1:46-55

And Hannah prayed and said,
"My heart exults in the LORD;
my horn is exalted in the LORD.
My mouth derides my enemies,
because I rejoice in your salvation.

1 Samuel 2:1

Mary was probably a young teenager when Gabriel appeared to her and announced she was pregnant. Not only was she pregnant but the child she was carrying would be the son of God. Scared, she asked the angel, "How will this be?" And Gabriel told her that the Holy Spirit will come upon her. He also told her that a relative of hers, Elizabeth, an old and infertile woman, had also conceived a child, for nothing is impossible with God.

Mary travelled as quickly as she could to Judah to see Elizabeth. Upon seeing Mary, the baby in Elizabeth's womb, who would become known as John the Baptist, leapt for joy. Elizabeth told Mary that she would be blessed for believing that God's promise of child would be fulfilled.

That was enough for Mary to believe. She saw God's faithfulness fulfilled in Elizabeth and had faith that God was going to fulfil his promise with her. At this, Mary broke out in song.

The song is split into three parts. First she sings about how she can't help but rejoice. She isn't boastful about being used by God but praises God because he is using her. Then she says that God turns the world upside down. She was of a humble estate and now she was being exalted by God. Finally she says that this is God fulfilling his covenant.

This isn't a song that Mary knew and recited, this is a song that Mary couldn't help but sing after experiencing God. She came to know God and responded from the heart. When we experience God we should be like Mary and respond from the heart. Sometimes that might even mean bursting out in song.

Praise, praise the Father, praise the Son, And praise the Spirit, Three in One!

All Creatures Of Our God And King

1225, 1919

Words

St. Francis of Assisi

Paraphraser

William H. Draper

Music

Friedrich Spee

All creatures of our God and King,
Lift up your voice and with us sing,
Alleluia! Alleluia!
Thou burning sun with golden beam,
Thou silver moon with softer gleam!

O praise Him! O praise Him!
Alleluia! Alleluia! Alleluia!

Thou rushing wind that art so strong,
Ye clouds that sail in heav'n along,
O praise Him! Alleluia!
Thou rising moon, in praise rejoice,
Ye lights of evening, find a voice!

Thou flowing water, pure and clear,
Make music for thy Lord to hear,
O praise Him! Alleluia!
Thou fire so masterful and bright,
That givest man both warmth and
  light.

And all ye men of tender heart,
Forgiving others, take your part,
O praise Him! Alleluia!
Ye who long pain and sorrow bear,
Praise God and on Him cast your
  care!

Let all things their Creator bless,
And worship Him in humbleness,
O praise Him! Alleluia!
Praise, praise the Father, praise the
  Son,
And praise the Spirit, Three in One!

The heavens declare the glory of God,
and the sky above proclaims his handiwork.

Psalm 19:1

St. Francis of Assisi, otherwise known as the patron saint of animals, had a special bond with birds. As he prayed and walked through nature birds would come to rest on his arms and shoulders.

One day whilst traveling, a huge flock of birds gathered nearby and appeared to be watching him in anticipation. So St. Francis preached to them. He ended his sermon to the birds with, '...and always sing praise to God.' He wrote the poem that *All Creatures Of Our God And King* paraphrases as a meditation on Psalm 145. It is a call to all of creation to praise their creator.

Each verse ends with the refrain: *O praise Him! Alleluia!*, which emphasises 'the cosmic praise of all creation.' *[Psalter Hymnal Handbook, Brink & Polman, 1998]* It is a call for all of creation to lift their voices in praise.

Everything that God has made declares his glory but in modern life we don't really see much of God's creation. How much of creation do you actually see in the city whilst surrounded by concrete, metal and glass? Nature is hidden by architecture and the only wildlife you really see is the occasional pigeon.

14

God's creation declares his glory. It announces it. It affirms it. It proclaims it. If we take time to focus on what God has made; the stars, the trees, even the pigeons, we will see God's glory being declared.

Were the
whole Realm
of Nature mine,
That were an off'ring
far too small

When I Survey The Wondrous Cross

1707

Words

Isaac Watts

Music

Lowell Mason

When I survey the wond'rous Cross
On which the Prince of Glory dy'd,
My richest Gain I count but Loss,
And pour Contempt on all my Pride.

Forbid it, Lord, that I should boast,
Save in the Death of Christ my God:
All the vain Things that charm me
  most,
I sacrifice them to his Blood.

See from his Head, his Hands, his
  Feet,
Sorrow and Love flow mingled down!
Did e'er such Love and Sorrow meet?
Or Thorns compose so rich a Crown?

His dying Crimson, like a Robe,
Spreads o'er his Body on the Tree;
Then am I dead to all the Globe,
And all the Globe is dead to me.

Were the whole Realm of Nature
  mine,
That were an off'ring far too small;
Love so amazing, so divine,
Demands my Soul, my Life, my All.

And Jesus uttered a loud cry and breathed his last. And the curtain of the temple was torn in two, from top to bottom. And when the centurion, who stood facing him, saw that in this way he breathed his last, he said, "Truly this man was the Son of God!"

Mark 15:37-39

As a child, Isaac Watts complained about how poor the hymns they sang at church were, and how unenthusiastically the congregation would sing them. His father, the pastor of the church, said, "I'd like to see you write something better!"

Isaac Watts became one of the greatest hymnists of all time, with hundreds of hymns to his name. He transformed hymns, which were primarily sung Psalms and call-and-responses at the time, into popular evangelical songs full of complex theology that anyone could sing and understand. He believed that hymns shouldn't just be a recount of scripture but should make it alive and personal to those singing. He wanted people to have their own encounters with Christ through worship, and as part of that he rewrote a lot of hymns based on the Old Testament so that they also included the gospel message.

Watts set out to show that Jesus' death was relevant here and now. With this hymn he stands us before the cross and makes us reflect upon Jesus' death, so we can see how personal it is.

We shouldn't be content with how some non-believers view the crucifixion as an old, irrelevant or fabricated story. It should be our aim to reveal how relevant and personal it is, so that when they see the crucifixion their response is the same as the centurion's:

"Truly this man was the Son of God!"

O
for a thousand
tongues to sing

O For A Thousand Tongues

1739

Words
Charles Wesley

Music
Carl G. Gläser

O for a thousand tongues to sing
My great Redeemer's praise,
The glories of my God and King,
The triumphs of His grace!

My gracious Master and my God,
Assist me to proclaim,
To spread through all the earth abroad
The honours of Thy name.

He breaks the power of cancelled sin,
He sets the prisoner free;
His blood can make the foulest clean,
His blood availed for me.

He speaks, and, listening to His voice,
New life the dead receive,
The mournful, broken hearts rejoice,
The humble poor believe.

Look unto Him, ye nations, own
Your God, ye fallen race;
Look, and be saved through faith
    alone,
Be justified by grace.

See all your sins on Jesus laid:
The Lamb of God was slain,
His soul was once an offering made
For every soul in pain.

Glory to God, and praise and love
Be ever, ever given,
By saints below and saints above,
The church in earth and heaven.

And whatever you do, in word or deed, do everything in the name of the Lord Jesus, giving thanks to God the Father through him.

Colossians 3:17

"If I had a thousand tongues, I would praise Christ with them all," Peter Böhler said to Charles Wesley, who was inspired to write this hymn.

The original hymn consisted of eighteen verses, with the seventh starting with *"O For A Thousand Tongues..."* The first six verses were autobiographical of Wesley's experience of becoming a Christian but only appeared in the original publication.

This hymn is a great declaration of what Christ has done for us. The song proclaims the power Christ has over sin, the new life we experience being born again in Him, the abundant grace he blesses us with. It reminds us of the hope we have in Jesus but it also paints a portrait of a man who, after encountering Jesus, couldn't help but sing his praises, and even prays to God to assist him in proclaiming Christ around the world.

We don't have a thousand tongues to sing but we do have one. And though we can't sing with a thousand tongues at once, we can sing with the precious one that we do have.

Come Thou Fount Of Every Blessing

1757

Words

Robert Robinson

Music

John Wyeth

Come, Thou Fount of every blessing
Tune my heart to sing Thy grace
Streams of mercy, never ceasing
Call for songs of loudest praise
Teach me some melodious sonnet
Sung by flaming tongues above
Praise the mount, I'm fixed upon it
Mount of Thy redeeming love

Here I raise my Ebenezer
Here there by Thy great help I've
 come
And I hope, by Thy good pleasure
Safely to arrive at home
Jesus sought me when a stranger
Wandering from the fold of God
He, to rescue me from danger
Interposed His precious blood

Oh, to grace how great a debtor
Daily I'm constrained to be
Let that grace now, like a fetter
Bind my wandering heart to Thee
Prone to wander, Lord, I feel it
Prone to leave the God I love
Here's my heart, oh, take and seal it
Seal it for Thy courts above

Oh, that day when freed from
 sinning
I shall see Thy lovely face
Clothed then in the blood washed
 linen
How I'll sing Thy wondrous grace
Come, my Lord, no longer tarry
Take my ransomed soul away
Send Thine angels now to carry
Me to realms of endless day

Simon Peter answered him, "Lord, to whom shall we go? You have the words of eternal life."

John 6:68

Robert Robinson wrote *Come Thou Fount* when he was 22. As a teenager, his mother had sent him from their home in Norfolk to London to work as an apprentice to a barber. There he associated with a notorious gang of criminals and lived a life of depravity before meeting the evangelist George Whitefield, who inspired him to turn his life around and come back to Christ.

Possibly the most resonant line in this hymn is *'Prone to wander, Lord I feel it. Prone to leave the God I love.'* It's a line that was autobiographical for Robinson and rings true for too many of us. There is always something else other than God that is vying for our attention and once we turn our attention, we turn from God. But then Robinson concludes the verse by offering his heart to God and asking him to seal it.

When we find ourselves wandering from God, or something other than God seems more appealing, we should do as Robinson did and offer our hearts to the Lord for him to seal. For surely there is nothing greater, nothing more appealing, and nothing more worthy of our time than the Fount of every blessing.

Come Ye Sinners Poor And Needy

1759

Words

Joseph Hart

Music

Anonymous American Folk

Come, ye sinners, poor and needy,
Weak and wounded, sick and sore;
Jesus ready stands to save you,
Full of pity, joined with power;
He is able, He is able, He is able,
He is willing, doubt no more.

Come, ye needy, come, and welcome;
God's free bounty glorify;
True belief and true repentance,
Every grace that brings us nigh;
Without money, without money,
 without money,
Come to Jesus Christ and buy.

Come, ye weary, heavy laden,
Bruised and broken by the fall;
If you tarry till you're better,
You will never come at all;
Not the righteous, not the righteous,
 not the righteous,
Sinners Jesus came to call.

Let not conscience make you linger,
Nor of fitness fondly dream;
All the fitness He requires
Is to feel your need of Him.
This He gives you, this He gives
 you, this He gives you,
'Tis the Spirit's rising beam.

Lo! th'incarnate God, ascended
Pleads the merit of His blood;
Venture on Him, venture wholly;
Let no other trust intrude;
None but Jesus, none but Jesus,
 none but Jesus,
Can do helpless sinners good.

Come to me, all who labour and are heavy laden,
and I will give you rest.

Matthew 11:28

Despite growing up within a happy Christian family, and knowing the truth of the Gospel in his head, Joseph Hart didn't know it in his heart. He never let God's word take root and he soon succumbed to his temptations.

Years later he became aware of his sins and wanted to become a better man. Remembering the teachings of his family, he decided that he needed to believe in God but, like when he was a child, he never let the belief enter his heart.

He believed that it was his own action of believing in God that saved him. He made it about himself. He entered a period of doubt in his life where he was uncertain of his own salvation. Then, in 1757, he had an amazing vision of Jesus in the garden of Gethsemane, which showed him that Christ's sufferings were for him. He wasn't saved because he believed in God, he was saved because Christ died for him. In the two years that followed his conversion he wrote hymns with a sincere love of Christ.

It's a familiar story: a child in a strong Christian family grows up to denounce their faith, or lives a Christian life without ever personally knowing God.

This hymn reminds us that we can be certain that we can receive salvation through Jesus. It tells us to make sure we have true belief and true repentance and tells us not to wait for salvation but to receive it now.

Simply
To the cross I cling

Rock Of Ages

1775

Words

Augustus Toplady

Music

Thomas Hastings

Rock of Ages, cleft for me,
Let me hide myself in Thee;
Let the water and the blood,
From Thy wounded side which
  flowed,
Be of sin the double cure;
Save from wrath and make me pure.

Not the labour of my hands
Can fulfil Thy law's demands;
Could my zeal no respite know,
Could my tears forever flow,
All for sin could not atone;
Thou must save, and Thou alone.

Nothing in my hand I bring,
Simply to the cross I cling;
Naked, come to Thee for dress;
Helpless look to Thee for grace;
Foul, I to the fountain fly;
Wash me, Saviour, or I die.

While I draw this fleeting breath,
When my eye-strings break in death
When I soar to worlds unknown,
See Thee on Thy judgment throne,
Rock of Ages, cleft for me,
Let me hide myself in Thee.

The LORD is my rock and my fortress and my deliverer,

my God, my rock, in whom I take refuge,

my shield, and the horn of my salvation, my stronghold.

Psalm 18:2

Augustus Toplady published *Rock of Ages* in *The Gospel Magazine* as one half of a pair of related articles. The first article was about how Britain would never be able to pay back its national debt (At the time national debt was about 122 million pounds, which is worth about 1.7 trillion pounds in todays money and as of 2018 is the amount of national debt the United Kingdom still has) and the second article, which Toplady wrote, was about the magnitude of human sin and how it is impossible to repay it ourselves, which is why we need Christ.

Toplady said that the redemption to be had in Christ "will not only counter-balance, but infinitely over-balance, all the sins of the whole believing world."

It is in times of trouble, when we try to make it on our own and fail, or are scared of what the future holds, that we realise we need Christ.

We need a safe place to rest. *Rock of Ages* is a prayer to God. It is a prayer that declares that we cannot make it on our own and that we need Jesus. It is a prayer that asks God to protect us. So we can rest in the knowledge that our debt has been paid by Christ, not a little but overwhelmingly in full.

In its first publication, before the first stanza Toplady wrote:

> Yes, if you fall, be humbled, but do not despair. Pray afresh to God, who is able to raise you up, and set you on your feet again. Look to the blood of the covenant; and say to the Lord from the depths of your heart…

> *"Rock of Ages, cleft for me…"*

My soul is thrilled, my heart is filled

I Saw One Hanging On A Tree

Words
John Newton

Music
Edwin Othello Excell

I saw One hanging on a tree,
In agony and blood,
Who fixed His loving eyes on me,
As near His cross I stood.

O, can it be, upon a tree,
The Saviour died for me?
My soul is thrilled, my heart is filled,
To think He died for me!

Sure, never to my latest breath,
Can I forget that look;
It seemed to charge me with his
   death,
Though not a word He spoke.

My conscience felt and owned
   the guilt,
And plunged me in despair,
I saw my sins His blood had spilt,
And helped to nail Him there.

A second look He gave, which
   said,
"I freely all forgive;
This blood is for thy ransom
   paid;
I die that thou may live."

When he was reviled, he did not revile in return; when he suffered, he did not threaten, but continued entrusting himself to him who judges justly. He himself bore our sins in his body on the tree, that we might die to sin and live to righteousness. By his wounds you have been healed. For you were straying like sheep, but have now returned to the Shepherd and Overseer of your souls.

1 Peter 2:23-25

In 1764 John Newton became the priest of a church in Olney, Buckinghamshire. Olney was a market town with a population of about 2,000. Over half of the population worked in the lace-making industry, and were poorly paid and poorly educated. Newton wrote a collection of songs, including *I Saw One Hanging On A Tree*, for the people of his parish. The collection became known as the *Olney Hymns*.

I Saw One Hanging On A Tree brings you to the foot of the cross at Christ's crucifixion. It's an account that has been told and retold countless times and to many it has no personal meaning. With this hymn, Newton shows just how deeply personal the crucifixion was. And by having us singing it in the first person we see Jesus hanging on the tree and, more powerfully, it is to us that Jesus says, *"I freely all forgive; This blood is for thy ransom paid; I die that thou may live."*

It is all too easy to sing in church for the sake of singing, or to read scripture as though it's outdated, but scripture is alive and when we worship through song the words we sing today are as fresh and as important to God as the day they were first written.

We should try to view hymns and scripture through the eyes of those who wrote it. Then we'll see just how personal and relevant they still are.

**And his praises
shall prolong,
While I live,
my pleasant song.**

O Lord I Will Praise Thee

1803

Words
William Cowper

Music
Unknown

I will praise thee ev'ry day,
Now thine anger's turn'd away!
comfortable thoughts arise
From the bleeding sacrifice.

Here in the fair gospel field,
Wells of free salvation yield,
Streams of life a plenteous store,
And my soul shall thirst no more.

Jesus is become at length
My salvation and my strength;
And his praises shall prolong,
While I live, my pleasant song.

Praise ye then his glorious name,
Publish his exalted fame!
Still his worth your praise
    exceeds,
Excellent are all his deeds.

Raise again thy joyful sound,
Let the nations roll it round!
Zion shout, for this is he,
God the Saviour dwells in thee.

You will say in that day:
"I will give thanks to you, O Lord,
for though you were angry with me,
your anger turned away,
that you might comfort me.

"Behold, God is my salvation;
I will trust, and will not be afraid;
for the Lord God is my strength and my song,
and he has become my salvation."

Isaiah 12:1-2

William Cowper was one of the popular poets of the 18th Century, with both Samuel Taylor Coleridge and William Wordsworth among his fans. He suffered from depression and had attempted suicide three times. He spent time in an asylum in St. Albans after which he went to live with Morley Unwin, a retired minister, and his wife Mary.

In 1773 he suffered from an attack of insanity, believing that not only was he condemned to Hell but that God was demanding him to kill himself. Mary spent a year looking after him and helped him to recover.

Whilst living with the Unwins he met and became friends with John

Newton, the writer of *Amazing Grace*. After he had recovered he moved to Olney and attended Newton's church where he continued to write poetry and hymns inspired by the refuge he found in God during his mental illness. John Newton then asked Cowper to contribute to a collection of hymns he was compiling that became known as the *Olney Hymns*.

Cowper's struggle with suicide and insanity brings deeper meaning to his hymn *O Lord I Will Praise Thee*. It is a deep confession of sober joy. Cowper decided to praise God every day, even though, in the depths of his depression, he wanted to die. The line, *'Jesus is become at length, My salvation and my strength'* transforms from a nice surface-level Christian belief to an image of the unending fight he had with his own sanity and his struggle to stay afloat using the strength given to him by Jesus.

This is a hymn that seemingly fell out of popularity in the late 1800's, but it paints such a powerful picture of how a man's faith in Jesus brought him back from the brink of death that it is worth remembering today.

When life is at its most unbearable we have to keep our eyes focused on Jesus and, knowing that we can't save ourselves, let him be our strength.

**While millions
join the theme,
I will sing,
I will sing**

What Wondrous Love Is This

1811

Words

Anonymous

Music

Anonymous

What wondrous love is this, O my soul, O my soul,
What wondrous love is this, O my soul:
What wondrous love is this, That caus'd the Lord of bliss,
To bear the dreadful curse, For my soul, for my soul,
To bear the dreadful curse, For my soul.

When I was sinking down, Sinking down, sinking down;
When I was sinking down, Sinking down;
When I was sinking down, Beneath God's righteous frown,
Christ laid aside his crown, For my soul, for my soul;
Christ laid aside his crown, For my soul.

Ye winged seraphs fly, Bear the news, bear the news,
Ye winged seraphs fly, Bear the news,
Ye winged seraphs fly, Like comets thro' the sky,
Fill vast eternity, With the news, with the news,
Fill vast eternity, With the news.

To God, and to the Lamb, I will sing, I will sing,
To God, and to the Lamb, I will sing,
To God, and to the Lamb, And the great I AM,
While millions join the theme, I will sing, I will sing,
While millions join the theme, I will sing.

Come friends of Zion's King, Join the praise, join the praise,
Come friends of Zion's King, Join the praise:
Come friends of Zion's King, With hearts, and voices sing,
And strike each tuneful string, In his praise, in his praise;
And strike each tuneful string, In his praise.

Thus while from death we're free, We'll sing on, we'll sing on,
Thus while from death we're free, We'll sing on;
Thus while from death we're free, We'll sing and joyful be,
And thro' eternity, We'll sing on, we'll sing on;
And thro' eternity, We'll sing on.

And when to that bright world, We arise, we arise,
And when to that bright world, We arise;
When to that world we go, Free from all pain, and woe,
We'll join the happy throng, And sing on, and sing on,
We'll join the happy throng, And sing on.

Your dead shall live; their bodies shall rise. You who dwell in the dust, awake and sing for joy!

Isaiah 26:19

What Wondrous Love has its roots in the oral tradition, being passed on without ever being written down. William Walker, an American Baptist song leader nicknamed Singing Billy, discovered the song whilst travelling through Appalachia. He then published it in his hymnal, *Southern Harmony*, and from there its popularity spread.

As the author remains anonymous, and the hymn started as a folk song, the words may have changed over the years as it was sung and taught by new communities. By finally publishing it, Walker somewhat cemented the words we have today.

The repetitive nature of the song serves two purposes. Firstly, it is much easier to teach and pass on a repetitive song orally as there are fewer words to remember. The second purpose becomes apparent whilst singing the song. Each time you repeat, *'What wondrous love is this?'* it becomes more meaningful. The repetition hammers the author's point home: this love is wondrous, and we don't deserve it.

The song tells the story of life after accepting Christ. First we receive God's love, then we are lifted out of the pit that we are sinking into, then we lift our praises to heaven, we declare that we will praise

God and see the millions of other believers around us, then we die with joy as we have been saved, and arrive in Heaven to sing on. It's the natural progression of a Christian's life.

The hymn starts by questioning how powerful the love that lead to the crucifixion is. The author comes to the conclusion that the only true response to experiencing such a wondrous love is to sing. Sing to God. Sing with other believers. Not even death can stop the singing of someone who has experienced God's wondrous love.

Holy Holy Holy

1826

Words

Reginald Heber

Music

John Bacchus Dykes

Holy, Holy, Holy! Lord God Almighty!
Early in the morning our song shall rise to Thee.
Holy, Holy, Holy! Merciful and mighty!
God in three persons, blessed Trinity!

Holy, Holy, Holy! All the saints adore Thee,
casting down their golden crowns around the glassy sea;
cherubim and seraphim falling down before Thee,
which wert and art and evermore shalt be.

Holy, Holy, Holy! though the darkness hide Thee,
though the eye made blind by sin Thy glory may not see,
only Thou art holy; there is none beside Thee,
perfect in pow'r, in love, and purity.

Holy, Holy, Holy! Lord God Almighty!
All Thy works shall praise Thy name in earth and sky and sea.
Holy, Holy, Holy! Merciful and mighty!
God in three persons, blessed Trinity.

And around the throne, on each side of the throne, are four living creatures, full of eyes in front and behind: the first living creature like a lion, the second living creature like an ox, the third living creature with the face of a man, and the fourth living creature like an eagle in flight. And the four living creatures, each of them with six wings, are full of eyes all around and within, and day and night they never cease to say,

"Holy, holy, holy, is the Lord God Almighty,
who was and is and is to come!"

Revelation 4:6-8

Reginald Heber had poetry in his veins. At the age of 17 he went to Oxford university, where he won awards for his poetry. He served as the rector of his father's church for 16 years and then, when he was 40 years old, he achieved his life-long dream of becoming the Bishop of Calcutta, in India, where he spent three years preaching the gospel before he died.

His hymn, *Holy Holy Holy*, isn't a song in and of itself, but it's an invitation to join in singing an eternal song. Both Isaiah and Revelations reveal visions of heavenly creatures endlessly singing, *'Holy, Holy, Holy, is the Lord God Almighty...'*

We are not alone in our walk with Jesus, we are not alone in our mission to spread the Gospel, and we are not alone when we raise our voices to sing worship to God. There are people all over the world, in the past, present and future, on Earth and in Heaven, who are worshipping God. So let us join together in endless praise, now and forever.

On Christ,
the solid Rock,
I stand;
All other ground
is sinking sand.

My Help Is Built On Nothing Less

Words

Edward Mote

Music

William B. Bradbury

My hope is built on nothing less
Than Jesus' blood and righteousness;
I dare not trust the sweetest frame,
But wholly lean on Jesus' name.
On Christ, the solid Rock, I stand;
All other ground is sinking sand.

When darkness veils His lovely face,
I rest on His unchanging grace;
In every high and stormy gale
My anchor holds within the veil.
On Christ, the solid Rock, I stand;
All other ground is sinking sand.

His oath, His covenant, and blood
Support me in the whelming flood;
When every earthly prop gives way,
He then is all my Hope and Stay.
On Christ, the solid Rock, I stand;
All other ground is sinking sand.

When He shall come with trumpet
    sound,
Oh, may I then in Him be found,
Clothed in His righteousness alone,
Faultless to stand before the throne!
On Christ, the solid Rock, I stand;
All other ground is sinking sand.

And the rain fell, and the floods came, and the winds blew and beat on that house, but it did not fall, because it had been founded on the rock.

Matthew 7:25

Edward Mote became a minister late in life. One day, a friend asked Mote to see his wife on her deathbed. He asked him to sing a hymn, as was customary. Unable to find his hymnbook, Mote pulled out the first few verses of this hymn from his pocket, which he had written down the week before, and sang them for the dying woman. She enjoyed the hymn so much that Mote left a copy with her. That evening, by his fireplace, he composed the last two verses.

This hymn becomes more profound knowing that it was inspired in part by a woman's final moments. She had lived her life with Christ as her solid Rock and soon she would stand faultless before His throne.

The hymn is based on the parable of the wise and foolish builders (Matthew 7:24-27). The foolish builder built his house on sand whilst the wise builder built his house on the rock. The foolish builder is the person who listens to what Jesus says but ignores him whilst the wise builder is the person who listens to what Jesus says and trusts him.

By trusting in Jesus and following his teachings we can be like the wise man. If our life is built upon the firm foundation of Jesus Christ then we will be saved in life and in death.

Still all my song shall be, nearer, my God to Thee

Nearer, My God, To Thee

1841

Words

Sarah Flower Adams

Music

Lowell Mason

Nearer, my God, to Thee, nearer to Thee!
E'en though it be a cross that raiseth me,
Still all my song shall be, nearer, my God, to Thee.
Nearer, my God, to Thee, nearer to Thee!

Though like the wanderer, the sun gone down,
Darkness be over me, my rest a stone;
Yet in my dreams I'd be nearer, my God, to Thee.
Nearer, my God, to Thee, nearer to Thee!

There let the way appear, steps unto Heav'n;
All that Thou sendest me, in mercy giv'n;
Angels to beckon me nearer, my God, to Thee.
Nearer, my God, to Thee, nearer to Thee!

Then, with my waking thoughts bright with Thy praise,
Out of my stony griefs Bethel I'll raise;
So by my woes to be nearer, my God, to Thee.
Nearer, my God, to Thee, nearer to Thee!

Or, if on joyful wing cleaving the sky,
Sun, moon, and stars forgot, upward I'll fly,
Still all my song shall be, nearer, my God, to Thee.
Nearer, my God, to Thee, nearer to Thee!

"Behold, I am with you and will keep you wherever you go, and will bring you back to this land. For I will not leave you until I have done what I have promised you."

Genesis 28:15

Sarah Adams was a poet from Harlow, England. In 1841 she wrote a collection of hymns for a hymnbook that the pastor of her church was collating. *Nearer, my God*, to Thee was one of them.

Verse one introduces the central theme of the hymn, to be nearer to God, and roots it in Christ before venturing back to Genesis for the next three verses. Verses two to four are based on Jacob's dream (Genesis 28), where he had a vision of a ladder leading up to heaven and subsequently founded the city of Bethel in the same location to be nearer to God. The final verse looks to the future.

Accounts from survivors of the Titanic have said that the ship's band played this hymn as they sank, although it was likely to have been to one of the hymn's alternate tunes.

Whether we are building a place to live, as Jacob was, or facing death, as the band upon the Titanic were, we should strive to be nearer to God and let not even death stand in the way.

Oh, Holy Night

1847

Words

Placide Cappeau

Translator

John Sullivan Dwight

Music

Adolphe Adam

O holy night! the stars are brightly shining;
It is the night of the dear Saviour's birth.
Long lay the world in sin and error pining,
Till he appeared and the soul felt its worth.
A thrill of hope - the weary world rejoices,
For yonder breaks a new and glorious morn!
Fall on your knees!
O hear the angel voices!
O night divine, O night when Christ was born!
O night, O holy night, O night divine!

Led by the light of faith serenely beaming,
With glowing hearts by his cradle we stand.
So led by light of a star sweetly gleaming,
Here came the Wise Men from Orient land.
The King of kings lay thus in lowly manger,
In all our trials born to be our Friend.
He knows our need-- to our weakness is no stranger.
Behold your King, before him lowly bend!
Behold your King, before him lowly bend!

Truly he taught us to love one another;
His law is love and his gospel is peace.
Chains shall he break, for the slave is our brother,
And in his name all oppression shall cease.
Sweet hymns of joy in grateful chorus raise we;
Let all within us praise his holy name.
Christ is the Lord! O praise his name forever!
His pow'r and glory evermore proclaim!
His pow'r and glory evermore proclaim!
His pow'r and glory evermore proclaim!

"This is my commandment, that you love one another as I have loved you."

John 15:12

Placide Cappeau, a French wine merchant and poet, was asked to write a poem by his parish priest for Christmas Mass. Even though his faith was dwindling, he agreed and wrote the poem on a coach journey whilst travelling to Paris.

When he had finished writing he realised that this was more than a poem and deserved music. He asked his friend, Adolphe Adam, to compose the tune to which he accepted but when Adam received the words he was challenged. Adam was a Jew. He didn't believe in the Saviour that Cappeau had written about, but despite that he composed the music anyway.

The priest, his church, and the whole of France fell in love with this new song but the love was short lived. After it was discovered that the composer was Jewish, and Cappeau had turned his back on religion, the song was banned by the church. The hymn was loved so much that the people of France ignored the ban and sang it in the privacy of their own homes.

In 1855 John Dwight translated the song into English. He was fighting for the abolition of slavery and was moved by the third verse, *'Truly he taught us to love one another... Chains shall break, for the slave is our brother...'* It became incredibly popular in the North during the American Civil War.

On Christmas day in 1870 during the Franco-Prussian war, whilst the French were fighting the Germans, a French solider stepped out of his trench without a weapon in his hands and sang the hymn. Instead of shooting, a German soldier stepped out from his hiding place and sang his own hymn in German, resulting in a cease-fire for the rest of Christmas day.

Christ's words have power. They had power when he first spoke them, they had power in the 1800's and they have power today. Despite the hymn being written by a non-Christian and composed by a Jew, Christ's own words, *'...love one another...'* pierce through the melody and bring peace. Jesus's words had the power to bring the dead back to life and the power to bring ceasefire to a war almost 2000 years later.

Jesus's words have power and when He speaks, we should listen.

Angels We Have Heard On High

1862

Words

James Chadwick

Original French

François-Auguste Gevaert

Adaptation

Henri Hemy

Tune

Edward Shippen Barnes

Angels we have heard on high,
sweetly singing o'er the plains,
and the mountains in reply
echoing their joyous strains:

Gloria, in excelsis Deo!
Gloria, in excelsis Deo!

Shepherds, why this jubilee?
Why your joyous strains prolong?
What the gladsome tidings be
which inspire your heav'nly song?

Come to Bethlehem and see
Him whose birth the angels sing;
come, adore on bended knee
Christ the Lord, the new-born King.

See within a manger laid
Jesus, Lord of heaven and earth!
Mary, Joseph, lend your aid,
sing with us our Saviour's birth.

And suddenly there was with the angel a multitude of the heavenly
host praising God and saying, "Glory to God in the highest,
and on earth peace among those with whom he is pleased!"

Luke 2:13-14

James Chadwick, whom this hymn is most commonly attributed, based it off of the French song *Les Anges Dans Nos Campagnes (The Angels In Our Countrysides)* by François-Auguste Gevaert. Chadwick's hymn is a loose translation of Gevaert's, mainly following the same structure and events as written in Luke's gospel.

The French Hymn tells the story of the Shepherd's after the angels had appeared to them to announce the birth of Jesus and on their way to Bethlehem. It was originally eight verses long, alternating between the Shepherds speaking and the women with whom they were speaking. They had heard this miraculous news of a saviour and were so excited about the news that the women had to ask them why they were so jubilant.

We should be like the shepherds. We should be so excited about Christ that people can't help but notice and ask us about it. Unlike the shepherd's on that day, we now know who that child was and what he has done. In light of that we should be even more jubilant in exclaiming *Gloria, in exelsis Deo! Glory to God in the highest!*

Jesus Paid It All

1865

Words

Elvina Mable Hall

Music

John. T. Grape

I hear the Saviour say,
"Thy strength indeed is small;
Child of weakness, watch and pray,
Find in Me thine all in all."

Jesus paid it all,
All to Him I owe;
Sin had left a crimson stain,
He washed it white as snow.

For nothing good have I
Whereby Thy grace to claim;
I'll wash my garments white
In the blood of Calv'ry's Lamb.

And now complete in Him,
My robe, His righteousness,
Close sheltered 'neath His side,
I am divinely blest.

Lord, now indeed I find
Thy pow'r, and Thine alone,
Can change the leper's spots
And melt the heart of stone.

When from my dying bed
My ransomed soul shall rise,
"Jesus died my soul to save,"
Shall rend the vaulted skies.

And when before the throne
I stand in Him complete,
I'll lay my trophies down,
All down at Jesus' feet.

"Watch and pray that you may not enter into temptation. The spirit indeed is willing, but the flesh is weak."

Mark 14:38

Whilst sitting in the choir stalls during church, Elvina Hall found herself questioning her deservedness of salvation and the price Jesus paid for it. She felt words forming in her mind and, in a hurry to jot them down she scribbled them upon a page in her hymnbook. After the service she showed them to her pastor who told her that John Grape, their organist had approached him that same day with a new tune he had composed. Hall's words and Grape's melody fitted together perfectly.

The first verse of the hymn echoes the words that Jesus said to Peter before he was betrayed. Peter was unable to stay awake and stand guard whilst Jesus prayed. Three times, Jesus asked him, and three times he failed. The remaining verses and the chorus of the hymn then become our prayer to Jesus, acknowledging that we cannot earn our salvation but that Jesus has paid for our salvation.

As Christians we want to serve Christ wholly, but as humans we find ourselves frequently failing. This hymn serves to remind us that even in our weakest moments, when we are sleeping instead of doing Jesus' will, Jesus still paid for our sins. It is a sober reminder that we owe Jesus everything.

O come
to the Father,
Thro' Jesus the son

To God Be The Glory

1870

Words

Fanny Crosby

Tune

William Howard Doane

To God be the glory, great things he hath done,
So loved he the world that he gave us his Son,
Who yielded his life an atonement for sin,
And opened the Life-Gate, that all may come in.

Praise the Lord, praise the Lord,
Let the earth hear his voice;
Praise the Lord, praise the Lord,
Let the people rejoice;
O come to the Father, thro' Jesus the Son,
And give him the glory, great things he hath done.

O perfect redemption, the purchase of blood,
To every believer the promise of God;
The vilest offender who truly believes,
Most surely from Jesus a pardon receives.

Great things he hath taught us, great things he hath done,
And great our rejoicing thro' Jesus the Son;
But purer, and higher, and greater will be
Our wonder, our transport, when Jesus we see.

...to the only wise God be glory forevermore through Jesus Christ!
Amen.

Romans 16:27

To God Be The Glory was first published in a book of hymns published by William Doane, who also composed its music.

This hymn is a joyous shout of praise. It is a redemption song. It is an expression of utmost exaltation because of our redemption through Jesus Christ. The jubilation comes from the unburdening of our sin, like a heavy chain sliding from our shoulders.

Verse one shows God's glory through His sacrifice of His Son (John 3:16). Verse two highlights how perfect the redemption is. No one is spared from God's grace if they truly believe.

The phrase *'vilest offender'* is harsh and conjures up the image of a prisoner having committed the most horrendous crime. Crosby probably wanted it to leave a foul taste in our mouths. It's immediately followed by the words *'...who truly believes,'* which is so sweet that it washes away the foul taste left by that *'vilest offender.'* Crosby, who was blind from a young age, uses this to bestow a mini experience of salvation through one of her remaining senses: taste.

Verse three then brings us all together in great rejoicing through Jesus.

To God Be The Glory is a map that leads us to God, through Jesus. It is the journey of our personal transformation, through the pardon we receive from God. And once we have personally experienced God's grace, we can't help but give God the glory for the great things he has done.

Echoes of mercy, whispers of love

Blessed Assurance

1873

Words

Fanny Crosby

Tune

Phoebe Knapp

Blessed assurance, Jesus is mine!
O what a foretaste of glory divine!
Heir of salvation, purchase of God,
Born of His Spirit, washed in His blood

This is my story, this is my song,
praising my Saviour all the day long;
this is my story, this is my song,
praising my Saviour all the day long.

Perfect submission, perfect delight!
Visions of rapture now burst on my sight;
Angels descending bring from above
Echoes of mercy, whispers of love

Perfect submission, all is at rest!
I in my Saviour am happy and blessed,
Watching and waiting, looking above,
Filled with His goodness, lost in His love.

For to me to live is Christ, and to die is gain.

Philippians 1:21

Despite being blind from a young age, Fanny Crosby is one of the most prolific hymn writers of all time, having written over 8,000 of them. Although she is most known for her hymns and poems, she said that her calling and profession was that of a missionary worker in her city, Manhattan. Many of her hymns were written as responses to her missionary work. She had a great awareness of the needs of the immigrants and poverty-stricken in her home of Manhattan and dedicated her life to helping them. She said, "From the time I received my first check for my poems, I made up my mind to open my hand wide to those who needed assistance."

Blessed Assurance reveals how personal Crosby's faith was. It mirrors Pauls' words in Philippians 1, *'For to me to live is Christ, and to die is gain.'* Crosby lived as Christ. She was constantly helping those in need and donated the sales from her poetry to help them. She unashamedly lived her life in a way that always pointed to Christ.

This is my story: For Crosby, the story of her life was the Gospel of Christ. She never wanted her life to be about herself. If you asked her for an autobiography of her life, I imagine that she would just hand you the Gospels.

This is my song: Her life was an act of worship. Everything she did was to honour and glorify God. And her physical acts of worship, her missionary work, sang of her salvation in Christ, her blessed assurance.

To live as Christ means that we should constantly be pursuing Jesus and whatever we do should proclaim His gospel. When people look at your life do they see Christ first?

It is well,
it is well,
with my soul

It Is Well
With My Soul

Words

Horatio Gates Spafford

Music

Philip Bliss

When peace like a river, attendeth my way,
When sorrows like sea billows roll
Whatever my lot, thou hast taught me to say
It is well, it is well, with my soul

It is well
With my soul
It is well, it is well with my soul

Though Satan should buffet, though trials
    should come,
Let this blest assurance control,
That Christ has regarded my helpless estate,
And hath shed His own blood for my soul

My sin, oh, the bliss of this glorious thought
My sin, not in part but the whole,
Is nailed to the cross, and I bear it no more,
Praise the Lord, praise the Lord, o my soul

"'Is all well with you? Is all well with your husband? Is all well with the child?'" And she answered, "All is well."

2 Kings 4:26

This hymn was written after an unimaginable tragedy.

Horatio and Anna Spafford lost their first son, when he was only a toddler, to scarlet fever. Horatio was a successful lawyer who had invested a lot of money in property. The Great Chicago Fire of 1871 caused enough damage to ruin him financially. Amidst this dark period of their lives, Horatio and Anna thought it would be good to take their four daughters, the youngest just being two years old, on a holiday to Europe. Last-minute business problems meant that Horatio had to delay his departure but insisted that his wife and children start their holiday without him.

The boat they sailed on, the *SS Ville du Havre*, collided with another boat. All four children died. The youngest child was ripped from Anna's arms by the water. Horatio received a telegram from his wife who had made it to Wales, which simply said: *'Saved alone'*.

Horatio boarded the next boat to Europe. The captain invited him into his cabin and told him that they were now sailing over the spot where the boat had sank. Horatio, three miles above the wreckage, looked out over the spot where his daughters had drowned. He then returned to his cabin and wrote:

When peace like a river, attendeth my way,
When sorrows like sea billows roll
Whatever my lot, thou hast taught me to say
It is well, it is well, with my soul

That first verse is about as powerful and personal as they come. The imagery of the rolling sea billows takes a more profound meaning when you realise that they are the waves above his children's graves.

It is natural for us to question *why* it is well with Horatio's soul after such tragedy. But the answer comes in the second verse:

That Christ has regarded my helpless estate,
And hath shed His own blood for my soul

All is well with his soul because it has been purchased and saved by Jesus's crucifixion, and his response to that, in the midst of heartbreak, was to praise the Lord.

People use tragedies as an excuse to not believe in God. People who have professed a Christian faith for a lifetime have been known to renounce it in the aftermath of a tragedy. But tragedy doesn't change who God is, and it doesn't change what Jesus has done. Horatio Spafford had almost everything snatched from him but in the midst of it all he could still praise the ever-loving and unchanging God. And so should we.

Glory! Glory! This I sing

Nothing But The Blood Of Jesus

1876

Words
Robert Lowry

Music
Robert Lowry

What can wash away my sin?
Nothing but the blood of Jesus;
What can make me whole again?
Nothing but the blood of Jesus.

Oh! precious is the flow
That makes me white as snow;
No other fount I know,
Nothing but the blood of Jesus.

For my pardon, this I see,
Nothing but the blood of Jesus;
For my cleansing this my plea,
Nothing but the blood of Jesus.

Nothing can for sin atone,
Nothing but the blood of Jesus;
Naught of good that I have done,
Nothing but the blood of Jesus.

This is all my hope and peace,
Nothing but the blood of Jesus;
This is all my righteousness,
Nothing but the blood of Jesus.

Now by this I'll overcome—
Nothing but the blood of Jesus;
Now by this I'll reach my home—
Nothing but the blood of Jesus.

Glory! Glory! This I sing—
Nothing but the blood of Jesus,
All my praise for this I bring—
Nothing but the blood of Jesus.

For in him all the fullness of God was pleased to dwell, and through him to reconcile to himself all things, whether on earth or in heaven, making peace by the blood of his cross.

Colossians 1:19-20

Robert Lowry was a professor and Baptist preacher from New England. Even though he was an accomplished hymn-writer, Lowry said, "Music, with me has been a side issue... I would rather preach a gospel sermon to an appreciative audience than write a hymn." Which is probably why this hymn has the qualities of a good sermon: it has a concise message, that speaks gospel truth, and allows the congregation to respond in a personal way with God.

The response, *Nothing but the blood of Jesus*, flows through the hymn, hammering home the truth that we are saved by Christ's blood, and Christ's blood alone. It reminds us that we aren't saved by the good we do, but by the grace that came with the crucifixion.

We need to remind ourselves that there is nothing that we can do to save ourselves. Only the blood shed on the cross can do that. So stop worrying. Don't let the thought of your sin bring you down. You have nothing to fear. If you feel depressed or guilty because of your sin, know that the price of your sin has already been paid, and we are free from the hold that sin has over us because Christ died on the cross. Have peace and sing praise, for we have all been saved by the blood of Jesus.

O Joy
that seekest
me through pain

O Love, That Wilt Not Let Me Go

1882

Words
George Matheson

Music
Albert L. Peace

O Love that wilt not let me go,
I rest my weary soul in thee;
I give thee back the life I owe,
That in thine ocean depths its flow
May richer, fuller be.

O light that followest all my way,
I yield my flickering torch to thee;
My heart restores its borrowed ray,
That in thy sunshine's blaze its day
May brighter, fairer be.

O Joy that seekest me through pain,
I cannot close my heart to thee;
I trace the rainbow through the rain,
And feel the promise is not vain,
That morn shall tearless be.

O Cross that liftest up my head,
I dare not ask to fly from thee;
I lay in dust life's glory dead,
And from the ground there blossoms red
Life that shall endless be.

"Come to me, all you who are weary and burdened,
and I will give you rest."

Matthew 11:28

As George Matheson completed his studies at Glasgow University his eyesight began to deteriorate. He had an incurable condition that meant he was rapidly becoming blind. At university he had fallen in love with a woman he was hoping to marry, but when he told her that he would soon completely lose his sight she told him that she didn't want to be the wife of a blind man.

About twenty years later, the night before his sisters wedding, all of the anguish and heartbreak came flooding back and he rapidly wrote this hymn in a matter of minutes.

In times of distress it can feel like God has deserted us. He isn't answering our prayers and hopelessness rages like storm clouds within. This hymn reminds us that in these times God's love will never let us go and that God is providing for us a retreat and a place to rest and be restored in Him.

Tis So Sweet To Trust In Jesus

1882

Words
Louisa M. R. Stead

Music
William J. Kirkpatrick

Tis so sweet to trust in Jesus,
And to take him at his word;
Just to rest upon his promise,
And to know, "Thus saith the Lord."

Jesus, Jesus, how I trust him!
How I've proved him o'er and o'er!
Jesus, Jesus, precious Jesus!
O for grace to trust him more!

O how sweet to trust in Jesus,
Just to trust his cleansing blood;
And in simple faith to plunge me
'neath the healing, cleansing flood!

Yes, 'tis sweet to trust in Jesus,
Just from sin and self to cease;
Just from Jesus simply taking
Life and rest, and joy and peace.

When I am afraid,

I put my trust in you.

In God, whose word I praise,

in God I trust; I shall not be afraid.

What can flesh do to me?

Psalm 56:3-4

Tis So Sweet To Trust In Jesus was born out of a tragedy. Stead, with her husband and young daughter Lily, travelled from Cincinnati, Ohio to Long Island Sound, a tidal estuary between Connecticut and Long Island. One day at the beach, a boy was crying for help from the water. Stead's husband rushed in to help but as the boy clawed for help he pulled Mr. Stead under with him. They both drowned as Louisa and Lily watched helplessly from the shore.

Following her husband's death, Stead wrote this hymn. What a response to something so awful. There's such a tenderness and vulnerability in this hymn, which really shines above the tragic back-story. You can almost feel the agony Stead went through, after losing her husband, and the blanketing comfort she received from her faith in Jesus.

Life is abundant with heartache, uncertainty, and anguish and the more we try to overcome these troubles by ourselves the more insurmountable they become. In these moments all we can do is trust in Jesus, turn our fears and anxieties over to him and feel the relief as he lifts them from us.

All
to Jesus
I surrender

86

I Surrender All

1896

Words

Judson Wheeler Van DeVenter

Music

Winfield S. Weeden

All to Jesus I surrender,
All to him I freely give;
I will ever love and trust him,
In his presence daily live.

I surrender all, I surrender all.
All to thee, my blessed Saviour,
I surrender all.

All to Jesus I surrender,
Humbly at his feet I bow;
Worldly pleasures all forsaken,
Take me, Jesus, take me now.

All to Jesus I surrender,
Make me, Saviour, wholly thine;
Fill me with thy Holy Spirit –
Truly know that thou art mine.

All to Jesus I surrender,
Lord, I give myself to thee;
Fill me with thy love and power,
Let thy blessings fall on me.

All to Jesus I surrender,
Now I feel the sacred flame;
O the joy of full salvation!
Glory, Glory to his name!

Then Jesus told his disciples, "If anyone would come after me, let him deny himself and take up his cross and follow me. For whoever would save his life will lose it, but whoever loses his life for my sake will find it. For what will it profit a man if he gains the whole world and forfeits his soul? Or what shall a man give in return for his soul?

Matthew 16:24-26

Judson Van DeVenter was a musician and a school art supervisor from Michigan. He was an active member of his church and aspired to become an accomplished artist. His friends, who saw how gifted he was in his ministry, encouraged him to leave teaching behind and pursue full-time evangelistic work. He struggled between developing his talents as an artist and pursuing a life of ministry. He said, "At last the pivotal hour of my life came, and I surrendered all... I became an evangelist and discovered down deep in my soul a talent hitherto unknown to me. God had hidden a song in my heart, and a touching tender chord, He caused me to sing."

Each verse of *I Surrender All* shows the qualities needed to surrender to Jesus: Free will, humbleness, sacrifice, openness to the Holy Spirit, receptiveness to God's blessings. The final verse, which unfortunately is often omitted, shows what great reward God blesses us with for surrendering: salvation, and the joy that comes with it.

When Jesus called people to follow him, one disciple asked if he could first bury his father. Jesus' response was, *"Follow me, and leave the dead to bury their own dead."* (Matthew 8:18-22) Jesus believed that you should honour your parents (Matthew 15:1-9) but following him is more important than anything else.

We can live life enjoying the talents that God has blessed us with, we can follow Jesus and love our friends and family, but if we find ourselves having to decide between Jesus or something else then our choice has to be Jesus. For if Jesus has the words of eternal life, to whom else shall we go? (John 6:68)

God reigns;
let the earth be glad

This Is My Father's World

1901

Words

Maltbie Davenport Babcock

Music

Franklin L. Sheppard

This is my Father's world,
And to my list'ning ears
All nature sings, and round
  me rings
The music of the spheres.
This is my Father's world;
I rest me in the thought
Of rocks and trees, of skies
  and seas –
His hand the wonders wrought.

This is my Father's world:
The birds their carols raise,
The morning light, the lily white,
Declare their Maker's praise.
This is my Father's world:
He shines in all that's fair;
In the rustling grass I hear
  Him pass,
He speaks to me ev'rywhere.

This is my Father's world:
O let me ne'er forget
That though the wrong seems oft
  so strong,
God is the Ruler yet.
This is my Father's world:
Why should my heart be sad?
The Lord is King, - let the
  heaven's ring:
God reigns; let the earth be glad.

Look at the birds of the air: they neither sow nor reap nor gather into barns, and yet your heavenly Father feeds them. Are you not of more value than they?

Matthew 6:26

Maltbie Babcock was a minister from New York. He would often take long walks along the Niagara Escarpment where he would relish in the wide, sweeping views of upstate New York and Lake Ontario. Before he left for his walks he would tell his wife, "I'm going out to see my Father's world."

The original poem this hymn comes from was 16 four-line stanzas, each starting with, *'This is my Father's world.'* Babcock starts by showing how God's glory can be heard throughout the world and in the heavens: even the planets are using music to worship. Then he delves into nature with birds and lilies, which echoes Jesus' words in Matthew 6, "Look at the birds... Consider the lilies..." Then in the final verse Babcock acknowledges that this beautiful world isn't perfect but we have no reason to be sad because, no matter what happens, this is still God's world and he still reigns.

Though the central theme is that of nature declaring God, that final verse makes it personal.

Anxiety and stress can cloud your vision and make it hard for you to see past your worries, causing your worries to feel like a heavy rock within you. It's too easy to worry about what might happen, and focus on all the things that could go wrong tomorrow. Instead, look at what God is doing today. You'll quickly see that God's real blessings today outweigh any possible problems tomorrow. And when tomorrow becomes today, look at God's blessings again. Rest in the knowledge that, even though what is wrong can seem so strong, *God is the Ruler yet.*

**Thou
my soul's Shelter,
Thou
my high Tower**

Be Thou My Vision

6th Century, 1905, & 1912

Old Irish Words
Saint Dallán Forgaill

English Translation
Mary Elizabeth Byrne

Versified Text
Eleanor Hull

Music
Eleanor Hull

Be Thou my vision O Lord of my heart
Nought be all else to me, save Thou art
Thou my best thought, by day or by night
Waking or sleeping, Thy presence my light.

Be Thou my wisdom, Thou my true word
I ever with Thee, Thou with me, Lord
Thou my great Father and I Thy true son;
Thou in me dwelling, and I with Thee one.

Be Thou my battle Shield, Sword for the fight;
Be Thou my Dignity, Thou my Delight;
Thou my soul's Shelter, Thou my high Tower:
Raise Thou me heavenward, O Power of my power.

Riches I heed not, nor man's empty praise
Thou mine inheritance now and always
Thou and Thou only, first in my heart
High King of heaven, my treasure Thou art.

High King of heaven, after vict'ry won,
May I reach heaven's joys, O bright heaven's Sun!
Heart of my own heart, whatever befall,
Still be my vision, O Ruler of all.

Put on the whole armour of God, that you may be able to stand against the schemes of the devil. For we do not wrestle against flesh and blood, but against the rulers, against the authorities, against the cosmic powers over this present darkness, against the spiritual forces of evil in the heavenly places.

Ephesians 6:11-12

It is believed, although the original authorship is argued, that the monk Saint Dallán Forgaill wrote the original Irish words to *Be Thou My Vision* in the 6th century in remembrance of St. Patrick's faith. In 1905 Mary Byrne, from Ireland, translated the hymn into English. In 1912, Eleanor Hull, an English student studying in Dublin adapted and versified the hymn, which is now the most well known version of the song.

The hymn is a prayer asking God to equip us, prepare us and focus us for the spiritual battle we face. It's almost a spiritual cleansing, washing us of our Earthly ties and setting our focus and desire on what matters most to God. It's a hymn that demands to not merely be sung but to be roared from the depths of our hearts and lungs.

The fact that three different people connected with the hymn so much that they each felt God calling them to write, translate, and rewrite it shows how powerful its message is. It's a message that was as relevant 500 years ago as it is today.

God doesn't call us when we're ready. He didn't wait for Noah to learn ark-building before he told him to build an ark. God calls us when *He's* ready and that's when we have to ask Him to prepare us, equip us and make His desire our desire. He will never let us down.

My Saviour's Love

1905

Words

Charles Hutchinson Gabriel

Music

Charles Hutchinson Gabriel

I stand amazed in the presence
Of Jesus the Nazarene,
And wonder how He could
   love me,
A sinner, condemned, unclean.

How marvellous! how wonderful!
And my song shall ever be:
How marvellous! how wonderful!
Is my Saviour's love for me!

For me it was in the garden
He prayed, "Not My will,
   but Thine;"
He had no tears for His own griefs,
But sweat drops of blood for mine.

He took my sins and my sorrows,
He made them His very own;
He bore the burden to Calv'ry,
And suffered and died alone.

In pity angels beheld Him,
And came from the world of light
To comfort Him in the sorrows
He bore for my soul that night.

When with the ransomed in glory
His face I at last shall see,
'Twill be my joy thro' the ages
To sing of His love for me.

And there appeared to him an angel from heaven, strengthening him.
And being in agony he prayed more earnestly; and his sweat became
like great drops of blood falling down to the ground.

Luke 22:43-44

It is estimated that Charles Gabriel has written and composed around 8,000 songs under different pseudonyms. He taught himself music by playing the organ at his family home and began writing his own songs from a young age. The pastor of his church once asked Gabriel if he could recommend a hymn that would compliment his sermon the following Sunday. By the end of the week, instead of looking for a hymn, he had written his own.

Gabriel wrote *My Saviour's Love* having been inspired by Luke 22, in which Jesus goes to the Mount of Olives to pray before his arrest, and an angel appears to strengthen and encourage him. It's an account that only appears in Luke.

What does it mean to have a song? When Gabriel wrote, *'and my song shall ever be'* he was saying that he will always proclaim how marvellous and how wonderful it is to be loved by Jesus. It's an expression of the joy of salvation that comes from witnessing the torment and suffering that Jesus went through so that his love could be fulfilled.

What is your song and do others hear you sing? Are you singing about Jesus' love, or are you singing about something else?

And God sent us salvation
That blessed
Christmas Morn

Go, Tell It On The Mountain

1907

Words

Anonymous

Adapter

John Wesley Work Jr.

Music

Traditional African

Go, tell it on the mountain,
Over the hills and everywhere;
Go, tell it on the mountain,
That Jesus Christ is born.

While shepherds kept their watching
O'er silent flocks by night,
Behold, throughout the heavens
There shone a holy light.

The shepherds feared and trembled,
When lo! above the earth
Rang out the angel chorus
That hailed the Saviour's birth.

Down in a lowly manger
The humble Christ was born,
And God sent us salvation
That blessed Christmas morn.

How beautiful upon the mountains
are the feet of him who brings good news,
who publishes peace, who brings good news of happiness,
who publishes salvation,
who says to Zion, "Your God reigns."

Isaiah 52:7

Go, Tell It On The Mountain started life as an African-American spiritual song sung by slaves as they worked. It's unclear when it was first written but John Work, a choral director from Nashville, Tennessee, adapted the song and published it in his book *New Jubilee Songs and Folk Songs of the American Negro* in 1907.

There's a rich history of African slave songs, often known as Spirituals. They would provide a repetitive rhythm for their physical labour. The songs often used Biblical references that mirrored their history of slavery to inspire and motivate. Some of them even contained secret messages in the lyrics to help slaves escape, or escaped slaves stay hidden nearby. Whilst their songs were often about freedom from slavery, *Go, Tell It On The Mountain* reminded them that God had sent someone to free them and that salvation is something that needs to be shared far and wide.

When the angels told the shepherds the good news of great joy it was a promise of salvation to come. After his resurrection, Jesus told his followers to make disciples of all nations as that promise had been fulfilled. It doesn't always seem appropriate to share the Gospel, and sometimes it can feel difficult or awkward but the Gospel of Jesus Christ, and the joyful news of salvation that comes with it, deserves to be shared no matter what situation we're in.

Fill us with the Light of day!

Joyful, Joyful, We Adore Thee

1907

Words

Henry van Dyke

Music

Ludwig van Beethoven

Joyful, joyful, we adore Thee,
God of glory, Lord of love;
Hearts unfold like flow'rs before Thee,
Op'ning to the sun above.
Melt the clouds of sin and sadness;
Drive the dark of doubt away;
Giver of immortal gladness,
Fill us with the light of day!

All Thy works with joy surround Thee,
Earth and heav'n reflect Thy rays,
Stars and angels sing around Thee,
Center of unbroken praise.
Field and forest, vale and mountain,
Flow'ry meadow, flashing sea,
Singing bird and flowing fountain
Call us to rejoice in Thee.

Thou art giving and forgiving,
Ever blessing, ever blest,
Wellspring of the joy of living,
Ocean depth of happy rest!
Thou our Father, Christ our Brother,
All who live in love are Thine;
Teach us how to love each other,
Lift us to the joy divine.

Mortals, join the happy chorus,
Which the morning stars began;
Father love is reigning o'er us,
Brother love binds man to man.
Ever singing, march we onward,
Victors in the midst of strife,
Joyful music leads us Sunward
In the triumph song of life.

But rejoice insofar as you share Christ's sufferings, that you may also rejoice and be glad when his glory is revealed.

1 Peter 4:13

Helen Keller said of her friend Henry van Dyke: "Dr. van Dyke is the kind of a friend to have when one is up against a difficult problem. He will take trouble, days and nights of trouble, if it is for somebody else or for some cause he is interested in." Who wouldn't want a friend like that?

In this hymn, van Dyke takes time to notice the joys of creation around him - the stars, the forests, the sea - but he isn't blinded by joy. He prays for God to *'melt the clouds of sin and sadness'* and to *'drive the dark of doubt away.'* Whilst suffering, the glory of creation was revealed. And, in verse three, the glory of creation leads straight to Christ.

We don't have to feel happy to be joyful. Happiness is a fleeting emotion in the here and now. Joy is experienced when we encounter God – *'Lift us to the joy divine'*.

Van Dyke didn't wait for the clouds of sadness to melt before he adored God joyfully and neither should we. I believe it was van Dykes deep-set joy that made him the great friend Keller wrote about. He encountered God's joy and couldn't help but act out his love. And when he acted out his love, his friends saw Christ in him.

I will cling to
the old rugged cross

The Old Rugged Cross

1913

Words

George Bennard

Music

George Bennard

On a hill far away stood an old rugged cross,
The emblem of suffering and shame;
And I love that old cross, where the dearest and best
For a world of lost sinners was slain.

So I'll cherish the old rugged cross,
Till my trophies at last I lay down;
I will cling to the old rugged cross,
And exchange it some day for a crown.

O that old rugged cross, so despised by the world,
Has a wondrous attraction for me;
For the dear Lamb of God left his glory above
To bear it to dark Calvary.

In the old rugged cross, stained with blood so divine,
A wondrous beauty I see,
For 'twas on that old cross Jesus suffered and died,
To pardon and sanctify me.

To the old rugged cross I will ever be true,
Its shame and reproach gladly bear;
Then he'll call me some day to my home far away,
Where his glory forever I'll share.

Do not fear what you are about to suffer. Behold, the devil is about to throw some of you into prison, that you may be tested, and for ten days you will have tribulation. Be faithful unto death, and I will give you the crown of life.

Revelation 2:10

George Bennard, an evangelist from Ohio, started to write *The Old Rugged Cross* in 1912 in Michigan whilst reflecting on the importance of the cross. He finished it in 1913 in Wisconsin where he presented it for the first time.

The hymn is written in a way that draws us in. At first the cross is *on a hill far away*, then in verse two we see the *Lamb of God* bearing the cross, then in verse three we can see the blood stains before verse four makes it personal and reveals its heavenly context. In each verse we draw closer and closer to the cross as more of the miracle of Jesus' death is revealed to us.

The second lines of each verse are also connected. In verse one the cross is the emblem of suffering and shame but verse two juxtaposes it as holding a wondrous attraction. Verse three calls it a wondrous beauty, right after revealing the bloodstains. Verse four brings it full circle as it calls back to the shame mentioned in verse one, this time calling it a shame to gladly bear.

The cross isn't something to be seen from a distance but is something we should examine (and even bear [Luke 9:23]). When we contemplate the cross we see how brutal and how beautiful it is. It is a tortuous death that reveals a new life. The crown that the cross will be exchanged for is the crown of eternal life.

No matter what hardships we will face in our lives, we are called to hold steadfast to our faith in Jesus and the promise God has fulfilled in him. No matter how our lives change, for better or for worse, God remains the same and his promise never changes. So let's cling to the cross, gladly bear its shame until the day we die, so we can one day exchange it for a crown.

Now What?

Now that you've acquainted yourself with these hymns you might be wondering what you should do next. This is my answer:

Get to know God more deeply. Read the Bible, go to church, and surround yourself with friends who can encourage you in your faith.

Then worship. Praise with words, with music, with prayers. Learn these hymns. Sing them. Play them. Remember them. Use them to further your relationship with God. Then find other songs you can worship with: modern songs, old songs, or write your own songs.

And then go. Go out into your neighbourhood, your town, your city, and worship with acts of love. Love your friends, your family and your neighbours.

Let God change your heart. First you believe and then you act on your beliefs. Live and love in such a way that it reveals God's character to those around you, for this is pleasing to God.

Worship is not through music alone.
Your whole life is worship.
So go now and worship.

One Final Hymn

I was asked to lead worship one Sunday evening at my Church in Hertford. I love leading worship. I feel closest to God through musical worship (being in nature is a close second) so being able to lead people in worship and to help them feel that connection is both a blessing and an honour, and not one that I take lightly.

Whenever I lead worship I spend a long time praying and playing music before hand, searching for the right songs to sing and the right key to sing them in. I practice the songs until I feel like I can play them as perfectly as I am able.

On this particular Sunday I had chosen to teach my church *So Will I (100 Billion X)*, which is a fantastic song by Hillsong United. But no matter how much I practiced it I just couldn't get it right. That morning I was feeling really down and disheartened by it. I just didn't feel like my plan for the Sunday service was good enough. I stayed home from the morning service to work on it. Normally I'd spend that time rehearsing, but that morning I decided to just pray and read. In these situations I find myself turning to the Psalms.

I read Psalm 95, which says:

Come, let us sing for joy to the LORD;
let us shout aloud to the Rock of our salvation.
Let us come before him with thanksgiving
and extol him with music and song.

I then picked up my guitar and strummed chords as I read it. Then I started to sing it. I could feel God's presence with me as I was struck with inspiration. It felt less like a lightning bolt and more like slowly boiling water, gradually reaching a rolling boil and spilling over the sides of the pot.

I sang through the Psalm and then spent time writing my own song inspired by it.

When Jamie, my brother, came around after church I played it to him.

"You should sing it at church tonight," he told me.

So I did. I scrapped *So Will I (100 Billion X)* and printed off chords and lyrics to my own song. That evening when I greeted the band I told them that I had a new song that we were going to sing.

"How new is it?" someone asked.

"Oh, it was written this morning," I told them.

The band knocked it out of the park. They learned the lyrics and developed their own musical flourishes and harmonies to complement the song and we taught it to our church less than an hour later.

Our pastor spoke on the gifts of the Holy Spirit. It felt like a perfect harmony, discussing the Holy Spirit and sharing a gift the Holy Spirit bestowed upon me at the same time. God blesses us when we worship him, and when we worship him we bless God.

When you feel the Holy Spirit leading you, follow. Give in to God's inspiration. Feel encouraged to write your own songs, and don't feel afraid to share them with others.

The Greatest Of Gods

2018

Words

William Long

Let us sing, for Joy to the Lord,
Let us shout to the Rock of our salvation,
Let us come, before Him with thanks,
Let us praise, with the loudest of music and songs.

For he is the Lord, the greatest of gods,
And he is the King of all kings,
For he is the Lord, and he is my God,
For he is the Maker of all things.

Let us hear, the sound of His voice,
Let us see, the marvels of His creation,
Let us feel, forgiveness deep within,
Let us speak, of the wonders of His love.

In His hand, are the depths of the Earth,
In His palm, rise the peaks of the highest mountains,
In His breath, galaxies are born,
In His love, is the weakest of sinners, like me.

He is my God
He is my God
He is my God
He is my God
And I am His.

Bibliography

"101 More Hymn Stories." 101 More Hymn Stories, by Kenneth W. Osbeck, Kregel Publications, 1985, pp. 135–136.

Adams, Sarah Flower. "Nearer, My God, to Thee." Hymnary.org, hymnary.org/text/nearer_my_god_to_thee_nearer_to_thee_een.

Aitken, Jonathan. John Newton: from Disgrace to Amazing Grace. Crossway Books, 2007.

"All Creatures of Our God and King." A Dictionary of Hymnology: Setting Forth the Origin and History of Christian Hymns of All Ages and Nations, by John Julian, Dover, 1957.

"The Amazing Story of 'O Holy Night'." Stories Behind the Best-Loved Songs of Christmas, by Ace Collins, Zondervan, 2001, pp. 132–133.

Anonymous. "What Wondrous Love Is This." Hymnary.org, hymnary.org/text/what_wondrous_love_is_this_o_my_soul_o_m.

Brink, Emily Ruth, and Bertus Frederick Polman. Psalter Hymnal Handbook. CRC Publications, 1998.

Brown, Theron. "Missionary Hymns." The Story of the Hymns and Tunes, by Hezekiah Butterworth, Society for Promoting Christian Knowledge, 1874, p. 165.

Burden. "History of Hymns: 'Rock of Ages, Cleft for Me.'" Discipleship Ministries, United Methodist Church, 19 June 2013, www.umcdiscipleship.org/resources/history-of-hymns-rock-of-ages-cleft-for-me.

Byrne, Mary E. "Be Thou My Vision." The United Methodist Hymnal, The United Methodist Publishing House, 1989, pp. 532–533.

Child, Harold. "William Cowper." The Cambridge History of English and American Literature, XI, Putnam, 1907, pp. 1–8, www.bartleby.com/221/index.html#4.

"Come Thou Fount of Every Blessing." A Dictionary of Hymnology: Setting Forth the Origin and History of Christian Hymns of All Ages and Nations, by John Julian, Dover, 1957.

Cousin, John W. A Short Biographical Dictionary of English Literature. Dent, 1921.

Cowper, William. The Complete Poetical Works. 2nd ed., Oxford University Press, 1911.

Cowper, William. "There Is A Fountain." Hymnary.org, 2019, hymnary.org/tune/there_is_a_fountain_filled_with_blo_amer.

Donnachie, Ian L., and Carmen Lavin. From Enlightenment to Romanticism. Manchester University Press, Published in Association with the Open University, 2004.

Dyer, George. Memoirs of the Life and Writings of Robert Robinson. Forgotten Books, 2015.

Evan. "What Wondrous Love Is This." Etymology of Hymns, 9 Aug. 2012, etymologyofhymns.blogspot.com/2012/08/what-wondrous-love-is-this.html.

Fielding, David. "O Love That Wilt Not Let Me Go: A Hymn by George Matheson." Crich Baptist Church - Derbyshire, UK, 17 June 2016, www.crichbaptist.org/articles/christian-poetry-hymns/poems-hymns/o-love-that-wilt-not-let-me-go-george-matheson/.

Hart, Joseph, and David Alfred Doudney. Hart's Hymns. W.H. & L. Collingridge, 1882.

Hart, Joseph, and Hawn. "History of Hymns: 'Come, Ye Sinners, Poor and Needy.'" Discipleship Ministries, United Methodist Church, 20 June 2013, www.umcdiscipleship.org/resources/history-of-hymns-come-ye-sinners-poor-and-needy.

Hatfield, Edwin F. The Church Hymn Book for the Worship of God. Ivison, Blakeman, Taylor & Co., 1872.

Hawn, Michael. "History of Hymns: Famed Hymn Expresses Writer's Longing for Heaven." Discipleship Ministries, United Methodist Church, 22 May 2013, www.umcdiscipleship.org/resources/history-of-hymns-famed-hymn-expresses-writers-longing-for-heaven.

Hawn, C. Michael. "History of Hymns: 'The Old Rugged Cross.'" Discipleship Ministries, 30 Mar. 2017, www.umcdiscipleship.org/resources/history-of-hymns-the-old-rugged-cross.

Hawn, Dr. "History of Hymns: 'This Is My Father's World".'" Discipleship Ministries, 20 June 2013, www.umcdiscipleship.org/resources/history-of-hymns-this-is-my-fathers-world.

Hawn, Dr. "History of Hymns: 'To God Be the Glory.'" Discipleship Ministries, 20 June 2013, www.umcdiscipleship.org/resources/history-of-hymns-to-god-be-the-glory1.

Hawn, Michael. "History of Hymns: 'What Wondrous Love Is This.'" Discipleship Ministries, United Methodist Church, 3 Apr. 2014, www.umcdiscipleship.org/resources/history-of-hymns-what-wondrous-love-is-this.

Hopler, Whitney. "Saint Francis of Assisi's Sermon to Birds." Learn Religions, 3 Sept. 2018, www.thoughtco.com/saint-francis-assisi-sermon-to-birds-124321.

"It Is Well With My Soul." She Reads Truth, 11 Dec. 2014, shereadstruth.com/2014/11/12/well-soul/.

"Jesus Paid It All - This Hymn Was More than a Coincidence." Christianity.com, Salem Web Network, 28 Apr. 2010, www.christianity.com/church/church-history/timeline/1801-1900/this-hymn-was-more-than-a-coincidence-11630381.html.

"Joyful, Joyful, We Adore Thee." Hymnary.org, hymnary.org/text/joyful_joyful_we_adore_thee.

Julian, John D. A Dictionary of Hymnology. 2nd ed., Dover, 1957.

Keller, Helen, and Kim E. Nielsen. Helen Keller: Selected Writings. New York University Press, 2005.

Matthews, Diana Leagh. "Behind the Christmas Carol: Go Tell It on the Mountain ★ Diana Leagh Matthews." Diana Leagh Matthews, 30 Aug. 2016, dianaleaghmatthews.com/go-tell-it-on-the-mountain/.

Mohr, Joseph. "Carols Silent Night and O Holy Night." History? Because It's Here!, Weebly.com, historybecauseitshere.weebly.com/carols-silent-night-and-o-holy-night.html.

McCann, Forrest M. Hymns and History: an Annotated Survey of Sources. A·C·U Press, 1997.

Mumford, James. "It Is Well with My Soul: James Mumford." Vineyard Churches UK & I, 7 Mar. 2013, www.vineyardchurches.org.uk/vineyard-vaults/it-is-well-with-my-soul/.

Mumford, Lou. "'Famous Hymn Still Resonates.'" South Bend Tribune, 14 Sept. 2013.

Newton, John, et al. "I Saw One Hanging on a Tree, In Agony and Blood." Hymnary.org, hymnary.org/text/i_saw_one_hanging_on_a_tree_in_agony.

"Nothing But The Blood Of Jesus." She Reads Truth, 19 Oct. 2016, shereadstruth.com/2016/10/19/nothing-but-the-blood/.

"O For A Thousand Tongues To Sing (18 Original Stanzas)." Discipleship Ministries, 16 Aug. 2019, www.umcdiscipleship.org/resources/o-for-a-thousand-tongues-to-sing-18-original-stanzas.

"O Holy Night." Christmas Music Companion Fact Book, by Dale Nobbman, Centerstream, 2000, pp. 36–37.

Piper, John. "Meditation on the Magnificent." Desiring God, www.desiringgod.org/messages/meditation-on-the-magnificent. Originally written: 8 December 1980

Piper, John. "What Is Worship?" Desiring God, 29 Apr. 2016, www.desiringgod.org/interviews/what-is-worship.

Robinson, Robert. "Come Thou Fount of Every Blessing." Hymnary.org, 2019, hymnary.org/text/come_thou_fount_of_every_blessing.

Smith, Matthew. "Come Ye Sinners (or 'Hart, The Herald Angels Sing The Wrong Lyrics')." Matthew Smith Music, 17 Mar. 2005, matthewsmithmusic.blogspot.com/2005/03/come-ye-sinners-or-hart-herald-angels.html.

"The Surrendered Life Initiates Change." A God Sized Future, by Ron M. Phillips, Charisma House, 2012, p. 29.

Telford, John. The New Methodist Hymn-Book Illustrated. 5th ed., The Epworth Press, 1948.

"The Old Rugged Cross." Hymnary.org, hymnary.org/text/on_a_hill_far_away_stood_an_old_rugged.

"This Is My Father's World - Lyrics, Hymn Meaning and Story." GodTube, www.godtube.com/popular-hymns/this-is-my-father-s-world/.

Tillay. "History of Hymns: 'When I Survey the Wondrous Cross.'" Discipleship Ministries, United Methodist Church, 7 June 2013, www.umcdiscipleship.org/resources/history-of-hymns-when-i-survey-the-wondrous-cross.

"'Tis So Sweet to Trust in Jesus." Hymnary.org, hymnary.org/text/tis_so_sweet_to_trust_in_jesus_just_to.

Toplady, Augustus. "Rock of Ages, Cleft For Me." Hymnary.org, hymnary.org/text/rock_of_ages_cleft_for_me_let_me_hide .

Turner, Steve. The Band That Played on: the Extraordinary Story of 8 Musicians Who Went down with the Titanic. Thomas Nelson, 2011.

Watson, Richard, et al. Companion to Hymns and Psalms. Methodist Pub. House, 1988.

Watts, Isaac. "When I Survey The Wondrous Cross." Hymnary.org, 2019,
    hymnary.org/text/when_i_survey_the_wondrous_cross_watts.

Wedgeworth, Steven. "The Meaning of the Magnificat." Wedgewords, 14 Dec. 2014,
    wedgewords.wordpress.com/2014/12/14/the-meaning-of-magnificat/.

Wesley, Charles, and Susanna Wesley. "O For a Thousand Tongues." Hymnary.org,
    hymnary.org/text/o_for_a_thousand_tongues_to_sing_my.

Wesley, Charles. "O For a Thousand Tongues to Sing." Hymnary.org,
    hymnary.org/hymn/EH1982/493.

About The Author

William Long was born in 1987. He grew up in Hertford, UK, and has a BA in filmmaking from the University of the Arts London. He has played the guitar since he was five years old (because his parents wouldn't let him have a Gameboy) and plays in a band at Hertford Baptist Church, where he occasionally leads worship. He has volunteered as a Young Life leader, and as a youth group leader for his church, for over ten years. He now works full time as a film editor and has edited two feature films. He has published a feature article on film postproduction in *The Digital Video Book* for Future PLC. He has also written scripts for animated short films, which have been shown at festivals around the world. In his free time, he likes to make games and write stories. He lives in Stanstead Abbots with his wife Agnes, and two Khaki Campbell ducks called Chester and Marjory.

You can see more of his work at:

www.hymnsofnote.com
www.longfilms.co.uk
www.longgames.co.uk

Printed in Great Britain
by Amazon